Contents

Where would you find a seahorse? 4

What kind of a creature is a seahorse? 5

How many kinds of seahorse are there? 6

Which habitats do seahorses live in? 8

How does a seahorse's body work? 9

What do seahorses eat? 12

What is seahorse family life like? 14

How do seahorses protect themselves? 18

Are seahorses endangered? 20

What can we do to save seahorses? 22

How do we learn about seahorses? 25

Fact file 28

Glossary 30

More books to read 31

Index 32

You can find words in bold, **like this**, in the Glossary.

Where would you find a seahorse?

You are standing on a beach in New South Wales, Australia (see map on page 6), wearing a diving suit and a snorkel. In the water just offshore are White's seahorses. Today, you are going to try to find one. You slip into the sea and start swimming.

After about an hour, you finally spot a seahorse almost hidden among some sea plants. Now you know why it's called a seahorse. The creature's head looks just like a horse's head! But the seahorse's whole body is only about the length of a crayon. You take a closer look. It has a pouch like a kangaroo. And its tail is curled tightly around a sea plant, in the same way that a monkey uses its tail to hang from a tree. What a strange creature!

Most White's seahorses live among sea plants. But some have been found living on underwater nets used to keep sharks away from beaches where people swim.

SEAHORSES

Heinemann
LIBRARY

Elizabeth Laskey

www.heinemann.co.uk
Visit our website to find out more information about Heinemann Library books.

To order:
☎ Phone 44 (0) 1865 888066
▤ Send a fax to 44 (0) 1865 314091
▯ Visit the Heinemann Bookshop at www.heinemann.co.uk to browse our catalogue and order online.

First published in Great Britain by Heinemann Library,
Halley Court, Jordan Hill, Oxford OX2 8EJ,
part of Harcourt Education Ltd.
Heinemann is a registered trademark of Harcourt
Education Ltd.

Edited by Barbara Katz, Kathy Peltan
Designed by Kimberly Saar, Heinemann Library
Illustrations and maps by John Fleck
Photo research by Bill Broyles
Production by John Nelson and Viv Hichens
Originated by Ambassador Litho Ltd.
Printed by Wing King Tong in Hong Kong

ISBN 0431 18201 9
07 06 05 04 03
10 9 8 7 6 5 4 3 2 1

British Library Cataloguing in Publication Data
Laskey, Elizabeth
Seahorses. - (Sea creatures)
1.Sea horses - Juvenile literature
I.Title
597.6'798
A full catalogue record for this book is available from
the British Library.

Acknowledgments
The author and publishers are grateful to the
following for permission to reproduce copyright
material:
Cover photograph by Doug Perrine/Seapics.com

Title page, pp. 4, 7, 14, 15, 16, 17, icons Rudie
Kuiter/Seapics.com; pp. 5L, 10 Edward Lines/John G.
Shedd Aquarium/Visuals Unlimited; p. 5R Tom & Pat
Leeson/Photo Researchers, Inc.; p. 8 James D.
Watt/Seapics.com; p. 9 Ken Lucas/Ardea; p. 11 Bob
Cranston/Norbert Wu Photography; p. 12 David
Wrobel/Visuals Unlimited; pp. 13, 28 David
Kearnes/Seapics.com; pp. 18, 19T Fred Bavendam/
Minden Pictures; p. 19B Doug Perrine/Seapics.com;
p. 20 Guy Stubbs, Inc.; p. 21 K. B. Sandved/Visuals
Unlimited; pp. 22, 23, 24 The Rolex Awards for
Enterprise/Tomas Bertelsen; p. 25 John Makely/The
Baltimore Sun; p. 26 George Grall/National
Geographic Society; pp. 27, 29 Ken Lucas/Visuals
Unlimited

The publishers would like to thank Michael Bright,
Executive Producer, BBC Natural History Unit for his
help in the preparation of this book.

Every effort has been made to contact copyright
holders of any material reproduced in this book. Any
omissions will be rectified in subsequent printings if
notice is given to the publishers.

What kind of creature is a seahorse?

A seahorse is a fish. All fish, including seahorses, have certain features that are the same.

An unusual fish

All fish have **backbones**. A seahorse's backbone stretches from the bottom of its skull to the tip of its tail. All fish also breathe through **gills**. They all use **fins** to swim. If you look closely you will see that seahorses have all these fish features.

There is one other fish feature that you cannot see. Seahorses, like all other fish, are **cold-blooded**. This means that they cannot control the temperature of their blood. Their blood matches the temperature of the water that they swim in. If the water gets warmer or colder, then a seahorse's blood will also warm up or cool down.

These seahorses and this trout do not look much alike, but they are both fish. Each has a backbone, gills and fins.

How many kinds of seahorse are there?

Scientists know of at least 32 **species**, or types, of seahorse. Seahorses are found in all the world's oceans, except near the North and South Poles. It is too cold for them there. Seahorses do not like very deep water. They live near the coasts where it is shallow.

Seahorses are coming to the UK

The seas around the British Isles are becoming warmer, so fish that usually do not live here are beginning to turn up. The spiky seahorse has lived in the western part of the English Channel for some time. Now it is also found in the North Sea sometimes, and off the coast of Wales. The short-snouted seahorse, more commonly seen in the Mediterranean, has appeared in deep water around the Channel Islands. The first one to be found off the mainland was discovered near Plymouth in 1998.

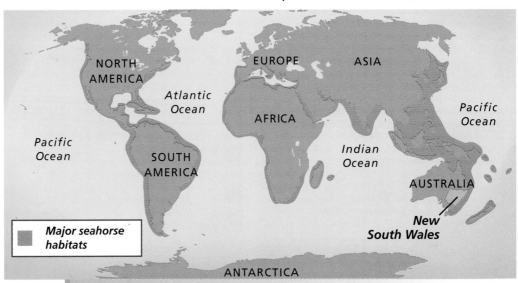

There are more species of seahorse along Australia's coast than anywhere else in the world.

At least ten species live in Australia

At least ten species of seahorse live along Australia's coast. One is the potbelly seahorse. It has a belly like a little balloon. Other interesting seahorses close to Australia are the pygmy seahorse and the zebra seahorse.

The pygmy seahorse is one of the smallest seahorses. It is about 2 centimetres long, smaller than your little finger. The zebra seahorse has black and white stripes like a zebra.

Potbelly seahorses like these can be white, yellow, or brown.

Some species live in other parts of the world

If you travel north of Australia, watch out for the thorny seahorse. It is covered with prickly spines! Further north, you might spot the tiger tail seahorse near the Philippines. It has a yellow and black striped tail.

If you are in southern Africa, you might see the rare Cape seahorse. It has a dark spot on its head and more spots on its back. Near Spain, France or England you might find the short-snouted seahorse.

Only four species of seahorse are found off the shores of North and South America.

Which habitats do seahorses live in?

Different **species** of seahorse live in different types of surroundings, or **habitats**.

Seagrass beds, coral reefs and mangrove forests

Species such as White's seahorse and the lined seahorse live in **seagrass beds.** Seagrass is a grassy plant that grows underwater. It often forms a thick 'forest' of grass. Seahorses wrap their tails around seagrass and may not move for hours!

The zebra seahorse and the pygmy seahorse live in **coral reefs**. Coral reefs are made of the skeletons of millions of tiny sea animals. Coral can have lots of tiny branches. Seahorses can hold on to these branches to rest from swimming.

The yellow seahorse lives in **mangrove forests** made up of groups of mangrove trees. Mangrove trees grow in shallow water along the coast. Mangroves' roots curve up and connect to the trees above the water.

The pygmy seahorse is very fussy about where it lives. Only a certain type of coral, known as a sea fan, will do.

How does a seahorse's body work?

When you look at a seahorse, you will see a few things that look familiar, like the eyes and the tail. Other body parts do not look familiar at all. The seahorse's different body parts help it to see, breathe, eat and swim.

The thorny seahorse's coronet can be clearly seen on top of its head.

The coronet is on top of the head

The little crown on top of a seahorse's head is called a **coronet.** Most seahorses have a coronet. Each seahorse's coronet is different from that of any other seahorse. The coronet also differs from one species to another.

The eyes stay on the move

Seahorses have two eyes, just like you do. Unlike you, a seahorse can move each eye in a different direction. It might keep one eye pointing forwards to look for food. The other eye might be aimed backwards, on the lookout for danger.

The snout sucks up food

The **snout** is a hollow tube like a straw. The seahorse uses it to suck up food. Snouts can be long or short. The short-snouted seahorse, as you might guess, has a shorter snout than most other seahorse **species**.

Fins are for swimming

Seahorses have two **pectoral fins** that look like little wings on each side of the neck. On a seahorse's back is the **dorsal fin**. These three fins help the seahorse to swim. Seahorses swim with the head pointing up and the tail curled. They move forwards by flapping the dorsal fin very fast. The pectoral fins also move very fast. They help the seahorse to steer and balance.

But seahorses are not fast swimmers. If a seahorse swam from one end of a bath to the other, it would take about five minutes.

To swim forwards, this Pacific seahorse can flap its dorsal fin 35 times per second.

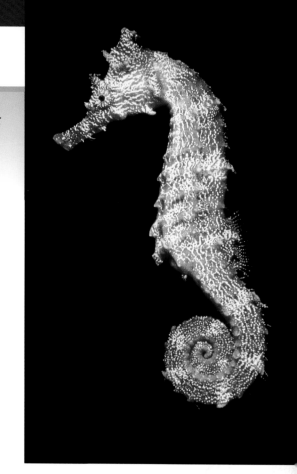

Seahorse tails curl in towards the front of the body, never away from the body. This is a thorny seahorse.

? Did you know?

If a seahorse wants to move up or down like a lift, it simply rolls or unrolls its tail.

Gills are for breathing

Just above the pectoral fins are tiny **gill** openings. The gills help seahorses to get oxygen from the water, so they can breathe.

The tail is for hanging on

Seahorses use their tails mostly for hanging on to a piece of seagrass, a bit of coral or even another seahorse! Because they are not very good at swimming, seahorses avoid doing it. This is where their tails are useful. Most fish swim around looking for food. Seahorses let the food come to them. They simply find something to wrap their tail around and wait for food to float past. When not wrapped around anything, the seahorse may keep its tail tightly curled.

What do seahorses eat?

For seahorses, dinner lasts all day. Most seahorses wrap their tails around something and spend the day eating the sea animals, called **zooplankton,** that float past.

Shrimp, shrimp and more shrimp

One favourite type of zooplankton are shrimp-like **crustaceans**. Huge numbers of these tiny animals live in **seagrass beds**. This works out well for the **species** of seahorse that live there. Seahorses have been known to eat more than 3000 of these shrimp between dawn and dusk.

This tiny crustacean is barely 2.5 centimetres long. Some larger seahorses can eat this shrimp. If the food will fit in the opening of its snout, the seahorse will eat it.

Seahorses have strong upper and lower jaws that can open and close the snout with lightning-fast speed.

When a seahorse spots a food item, it begins sucking the tiny animal towards its **snout**. As soon as the zooplankton enters the snout, the seahorse snaps the snout shut. The opening and shutting of the snout happens so fast that you probably would not see it. But you might hear a tiny click as the snout shuts.

No teeth, no stomach, no problem!
Seahorses have no teeth. They swallow their food whole. They also do not have a stomach. The food they eat passes through them very quickly. This is one reason why they have to eat so much.

What is seahorse family life like?

Seahorse family life is not like that of any other member of the animal kingdom. With other animals, it is the female who gets pregnant and lays eggs or has babies. With seahorses, the male gets pregnant and gives birth.

Seahorses go on 'dates'

A male and female seahorse spend a lot of time together before they mate. When they meet, one or both of them may change colour. Next, they may grab on to the same piece of seagrass or coral and spin around it for a while. Then they might leave it, link their tails together and swim back and forth together. Such a 'date' might last up to 9 hours. Most species of seahorse stay with the same partner for life.

These short-snouted seahorses can be found in some parts of the sea around the UK.

male's brood pouch

The female will look thinner after she puts her eggs into the male's brood pouch. The male will look fatter because his brood pouch will be full of eggs.

Males get pregnant

When two seahorses are ready to mate, the female puts her eggs in the male's brood pouch on the front of his body. The **brood pouch** is where the male **fertilizes** and then carries the eggs.

In many **species,** the female visits the male every morning while he is pregnant. The partners change colour when they see each other and twirl together around a piece of coral or seagrass.

Fighting for a partner

Sometimes more than two male seahorses can be interested in one female. When this happens, the males may fight. They might grab each other by the tail and wrestle. Or they might hit each other with their **snouts**.

Babies are born

Inside the **brood pouch**, the **fertilized** eggs develop into baby seahorses in two to six weeks, depending on the **species** of seahorse. During this time, the male slowly lets seawater into the brood pouch. This helps the growing babies get used to the seawater before they have to swim in it.

The male usually gives birth to the babies very early in the morning. He squirts the babies out of his brood pouch. This can take many hours. When he has finished, the male is very tired.

Depending on the species, a male seahorse gives birth to between 5 and more than 1000 babies at a time. Smaller species have fewer babies than larger species. The babies look like tiny adult seahorses. All baby seahorses are the same size. They are about 6 millimetres long, about as long as a grain of rice.

A group of baby seahorses is called a brood.

Babies grow up

Baby seahorses start eating soon after they are born. The opening in a baby seahorse's **snout** is only about the size of the dot over this letter 'i.' So they usually eat **zooplankton** that are not fully grown.

The father and mother do not provide any care or help to baby seahorses. In fact, very soon after the birth the parents leave to start another family. Many baby seahorses never grow up. Many end up as a meal for larger fish, crabs or seabirds.

Baby seahorses may find a place to hold on to soon after their birth, or they may spend some time floating freely in the water.

It takes small seahorses, such as the dwarf seahorse, about three months to grow up. Larger species, such as the White's seahorse, take six to twelve months. Scientists are not sure exactly how long seahorses can live. But they think that smaller species may live for a year and a half. Larger species may live for four to five years.

How do seahorses protect themselves?

Unlike baby seahorses, adult seahorses do not have many animal **predators,** or enemies. Seahorses have some tricks that they use to make themselves almost impossible to find.

They have bones and spines

Under their skin, seahorses have hard sheets of bone that protect their insides. The raised rings you see around a seahorse's body show where these sheets of bone join together. Sea creatures that try to eat seahorses usually end up spitting them out—too crunchy! After that, these creatures usually stay away from seahorses.

Some **species** of seahorse have sharp spines on their backs. Two examples are the thorny seahorse and the hedgehog seahorse. Most predators usually do not bother these prickly seahorses.

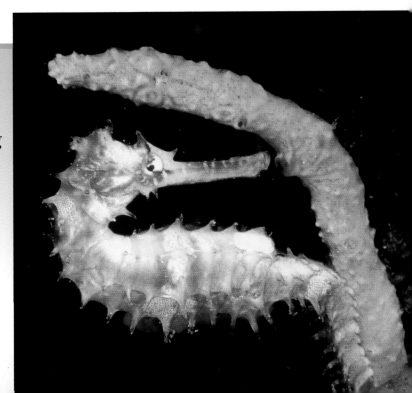

The spines on this thorny seahorse are long and sharp. They run from the top of the seahorse's head almost to the tip of its tail.

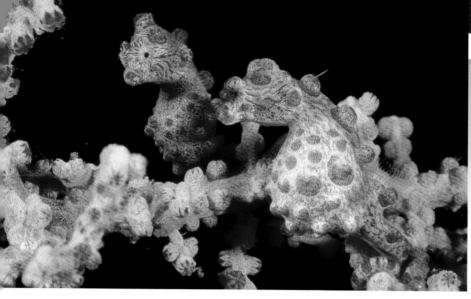

Some species, like this pygmy seahorse, change colour to match the coral they rest on.

They can blend into the background

A few predators, such as crabs, skates and even sea turtles, do not mind a little extra crunch. To keep from being eaten by these predators, seahorses can change colour to **camouflage** themselves. For example, a seahorse living in a **coral reef** can turn purple or pink to match the corals around it.

? Did you know?

It only takes a seahorse a few minutes to change its colour to match nearby plants or corals.

Pipefishes and sea dragons

Pipefishes and sea dragons are related to seahorses. They, too, are very good at blending in. Pipefishes look like straightened out seahorses. Their ribbon-like bodies look a lot like the flat pieces of seagrass they live in. Sea dragons look like seahorses that have grown leaves. The leafy bits make sea dragons hard to tell apart from a piece of floating seaweed.

Are seahorses endangered?

Seahorses' worst enemies are humans, not other sea creatures. Human activities harm and destroy the seahorse **habitat**. This is one reason why some **species** of seahorse may become **endangered**. Also, fishermen catch about 20 million seahorses a year. The seahorses they catch are used in medicines, made into **souvenirs** or kept as pets. As a result, the number of seahorses in the world's seas has fallen.

Seahorses can lose their homes

Putting up new buildings and cutting down trees along the coast can cause water pollution. This harms and destroys the **seagrass beds**, **coral reefs** and **mangrove forests** where seahorses live.

In 2001, the Cape seahorse became the first endangered species of seahorse. Building projects along the coast of South Africa have harmed its habitat.

These dead seahorses may be mixed with other ingredients to make medicines or used whole.

Seahorses are used in medicines

Some doctors in Asia use dead seahorses in medicines. Seahorse medicines are thought to help people with broken bones, breathing problems, heart disease and other health problems. Seahorses cannot have babies fast enough to replace the millions caught each year for these medicines.

Seahorses are made into souvenirs

For many years, gift shops in beach areas have sold keyrings, paperweights and jewellery made of dead seahorses. Each year hundreds of thousands of seahorses are caught and made into these souvenirs.

Seahorses are sold as pets

Seahorses seem as though they would make fun pets. But keeping a seahorse alive in a home **aquarium** is very difficult. Feeding them the right kind of food is one problem. They also get ill easily. Several hundred thousand seahorses are caught each year and sold as pets. Most of them die.

What can we do to save seahorses?

A group called Project Seahorse, based in Canada, is helping to save seahorses. Project Seahorse and other groups and individuals are working to help protect the seahorse **habitat**. They also help people understand the dangers seahorses face, and find ways to reduce the number of seahorses caught each year.

Protect the seahorse habitat

It is important to protect **seagrass beds**, **coral reefs** and **mangrove forests**. This will make sure that seahorses have a place to live. Protecting these areas may mean passing laws about what kind of building is allowed in coastal areas. Laws may also be passed to control logging and other activities that cause water pollution.

In 1996, scientist Amanda Vincent started Project Seahorse in Canada with her colleague, Heather Hall.

Some people in the Philippines now have jobs protecting seahorses.

Set aside safe places for seahorses

Setting aside an area along the coast as a safe area for seahorses can help. In these safe areas, or **sanctuaries**, catching seahorses is not allowed. This gives seahorses a secure place to have babies, and the babies can remain safe while they grow up.

At a sanctuary near the village of Handumon in the Philippines, people guard the water to make sure no one catches the seahorses that live there. Since this programme began, the number of seahorses in the area has been slowly increasing.

Doctors can help, too

Project Seahorse is working with doctors in Asia who use seahorse medicines. Sometimes other ingredients can be used instead of seahorses. Or doctors can try to use seahorse **species** that are less **endangered**.

These craft items are just some of the things made and sold by people who used to catch seahorses.

Stop buying seahorses

Many people who buy **souvenirs** like seahorse keyrings do not know that seahorses are in danger. Once people know this, most will probably not buy these souvenirs. Most people also do not know that pet seahorses usually die. If they did, they would stop buying them. This could save up to half a million seahorses each year. That is why educating people about seahorses is important.

Find new jobs for seahorse fishermen

What will happen to people who make their living fishing for seahorses? Project Seahorse is helping these people find other ways to make money. In the Philippines, some fishermen now make and sell crafts with seahorse designs.

How do we learn about seahorses?

Some scientists learn about seahorses by studying them in tanks. Others study seahorses in their natural **habitat**.

Scientists study captive seahorses

Seahorses kept in tanks need extra special care. The water cannot be too warm or too cool. The potbelly seahorse, for example, does best in very clean water that is 18 °C to 24 °C. The scientists also need to keep tanks full of live **zooplankton** to feed to the seahorses twice a day.

In the UK, the National Marine Aquarium in Plymouth has more **species** of seahorse than any **aquarium** in the world. It shows seahorses to the public, and successfully breeds many species.

Researchers at the aquarium are also studying how seahorses recognize and catch their food.

A scientist studying leafy sea dragons in an aquarium.

Scientists study wild seahorses

The first step in studying seahorses in their natural **habitat** is finding them. Once scientists find some seahorses, they may mark off the area with brightly coloured tape. This will make it easier to find the seahorses the next time. Then they collect **data** about the seahorses' size, weight and other things.

Scientists that study seahorses in the wild have to be patient. They might spend hours underwater watching one or two seahorses. They watch the seahorses to find out about many things. For example, scientists are interested in learning more about how seahorses mate. So they watch how seahorse partners act when they are together. Scientists are also interested in getting more details about how **species** of seahorse are different from each other.

Scientists put a little necklace with a number on it around a seahorse's neck. The number helps the scientists tell the seahorses apart.

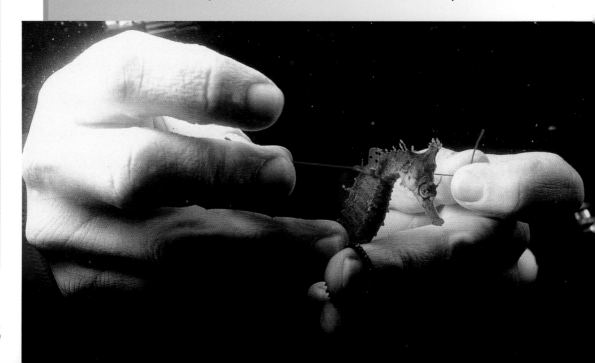

The natural beauty of seahorses is reason enough to work to save them.

We still need to learn more

There are still many things we do not know about seahorses, such as how they live and act in their natural habitat. Scientists need to collect more data to better understand how the number of seahorses has changed over the years. Scientists share what they learn with conservation groups and governments. Together they can work on the best ways to keep seahorses safe.

Seahorses are just one of the many creatures living in our seas. They are a tiny piece of the puzzle that makes up all life on Earth. All creatures on the planet depend on each other in one way or another. The loss of any species can affect others that depend on it. Working to make sure that seahorses do not die out is one way to help keep the puzzle from falling apart.

☑ The largest seahorse is the Pacific seahorse, which can grow to be 30 centimetres long.

☑ Seahorses, pipefishes and sea dragons are the only animal species in which males become pregnant and give birth.

☑ Seahorses can make a clicking sound by rubbing two parts of their skull together. The sound they make sounds like fingers snapping. Scientists are not sure why seahorses make these sounds.

☑ A yellow seahorse at the National **Aquarium** in Baltimore, USA, gave birth to a record number of 2020 babies.

☑ The Cape seahorse can live in water that is twice as salty as normal sea water. It can also live in water that has almost no salt in it.

The smallest seahorses are the dwarf seahorse and the pygmy seahorse. Both are less than 2.5 centimetres long.

✓ A sea creature known as a pipehorse looks a bit like a seahorse and a bit like a pipefish. Pipehorses have tails that curl and can grab on to coral or seagrass like a seahorse. But their bodies and heads are straighter, like those of a pipefish.

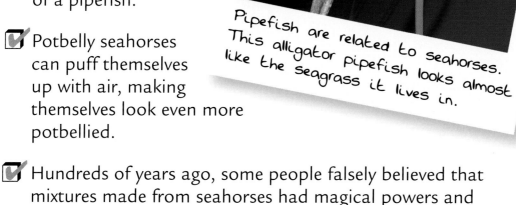

Pipefish are related to seahorses. This alligator pipefish looks almost like the seagrass it lives in.

✓ Potbelly seahorses can puff themselves up with air, making themselves look even more potbellied.

✓ Hundreds of years ago, some people falsely believed that mixtures made from seahorses had magical powers and could make a person go mad.

✓ The ancient Romans believed that Neptune, their god of the oceans rode through the waves on a horse-drawn chariot. So they thought seahorses were the babies of Neptune's horses.

Glossary

aquarium building where people can see sea creatures that are on display. Fish tanks are also sometimes called aquariums.

backbone bone that stretches down the middle of the back and protects the spine

breed when a male and female come together to make babies

brood pouch pocket-like flap on the front part of a male seahorse's body

camouflage to change the way something looks so it will be less easy to see

cold-blooded having blood that is the same temperature as the air or water an animal lives in

coral reef underwater formations made of the hard skeletons of millions of tiny sea animals

coronet bony growth that looks like a crown on top of a seahorse's head

crustacean type of animal that includes shrimp, lobsters and crayfish

data facts and information

dorsal fin fin on the back part of a seahorse's body. Seahorses flap their dorsal fin to swim forwards.

endangered in danger of dying out completely so that there will be no more left on Earth

fertilize make eggs able to grow and develop into babies

fin wing-shaped or fan-shaped part of a fish's body that the fish can move to help it swim

gill structure in a fish's body that the fish uses to breathe

habitat place where an animal lives in the wild

mangrove forest shallow area of water near a coast in which mangrove trees grow. Mangrove roots arch above the surface of the water.

pectoral fin one of two fins on each side of a seahorse's neck. Seahorses use their pectoral fins to help them steer and keep their balance.

predator animal that attacks and eats another animal

sanctuary safe or protected place

seagrass bed grassy plants that make up a thick underwater 'forest'

snout a seahorse's hollow, tube-shaped mouth

souvenir gift item that reminds people of a place they have visited

species group of animals that have the same features and can have babies with each other

zooplankton any of a number of very tiny sea animals that float in the sea and are eaten by sea creatures, including seahorses

More Books to Read

Awesome Oceans: Tropical Seas. Michael Bright. (Aladdin/Watts, 2002)

The Earth Strikes Back: Water. (Belitha Press, 2000)

First Look Through: Under the Sea. Claire Llewellyn and Angela Royston. (Heinemann Library, 1997)

Living Things: Seahorse. (Benchmark Books, 1998)

Index

babies 16–17, 28
backbone 5
birth 16, 28
blood 5
body 4, 5, 9–11
bones 18
brood pouch 4, 15, 16

camouflage 19
Cape seahorses 7, 20, 29
Channel Islands 6
colours 7, 15, 19
coral reefs 8, 19, 20, 22
coronet 9

digestion 13
dorsal fin 10
dwarf seahorses 17, 28

endangered species 20
eyes 9

females 14–15
fighting 15
fins 5, 5, 10
food 12–13, 17

gills 5, 11

habitats 8, 12, 19, 20,
   22, 26
head 4, 9
hedgehog seahorses 18

life span 17
lined seahorses 8

males 14–15, 16, 25
mangrove forests 8, 20, 22
mating 14–15, 26
medicines 20, 21, 23
Mediterranean Sea 6

National Marine Aquarium
   25

Pacific seahorses 28
pectoral fins 10
pets 20, 21
pipefishes 19, 28, 29
potbelly seahorses 7, 25, 29
predators 18–120
Project Seahorse 22, 23, 24
pygmy seahorses 7, 8, 19

research 25–27

sanctuaries 23
sea dragons 19, 25, 28
seagrass beds 8, 12, 20, 22
seahorse crafts 24
short-snouted seahorses 6,
   7, 14
shrimp 12
sizes 4, 7, 16, 28
snout 10, 13, 17
souvenirs 20, 21, 24

species 6–8
spiky seahorse 6

tail 4, 8, 9, 11
thorny seahorses 7, 11, 18
tiger tail seahorses 7

Vincent, Amanda 22

water pollution 20, 22
White's seahorses 4, 8, 17

yellow seahorses 8

zebra seahorses 7, 8
zooplankton 12, 13, 17, 25

Titles in the *Sea Creatures* series include:

Hardback   0 431 18204 3

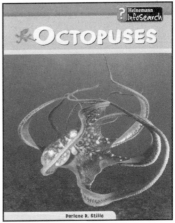

Hardback   0 431 18200 0

Hardback   0 431 18201 9

Hardback   0 431 18205 1

Hardback   0 431 18203 5

Hardback   0 431 18202 7

Find out about the other titles in this series on our website www.heinemann.co.uk/library